A Bitter-Swe

Living in the Amazing Grace of God

Dr. Coraleen F. Braxton

Living in the Amazing Grace of God
Leading Lady Publications
A Division of Anointed Word Media Group
1-800-597-9428
P.O. Box 35, Worton, MD 21678
www.publishyourchristianbook.com

Cover Design by: Tamika Johnson-Hall

ISBN-10: 0-9798084-1-3
ISBN-13: 978-0-9798084-1-8
LCCN: 2007905906

Printed in the United States of America

To order additional copies please contact:
Anointed Word Media Group
1-800-597-9428
info@publishyourchristianbook.com
www.anointedwordbookstore.net

Praise for Living in the Amazing Grace of God!

A life shared and poured out upon the altar that others may laugh, cry, identify, learn and be reminded that victory lies in applying God's Word to the circumstances of life. There lies victory as we choose an attitude of forgiveness and faith in God. Delightful reading and highly recommended for its clarity in relating what God can do, is doing and will do through a life submitted to "Him!"**Corinthia R. Boone Ph.D. Int'l Christian Host Coalition & Together In Ministry Int'l – Founder & President Capital Region National Day Prayer Chairperson**

I believe that Coraleen has tapped into a place that helps us laugh while we walk through the hallways of our heart and remove clutter. She shares by the leading of the Holy Spirit insightful ways that God dealt with her to bring about wholeness and healing like that of refreshing waters. I recommend this book and believe it is a tool God will use to help many experience the amazing grace of God!! **Dr. Decker H. Tapscott, Sr. Founder & Senior Pastor of Faith Christian Church & Int'l Outreach Center & Author**

Excellent work! This is a well-crafted array of insightful thoughts. A tapestry of spiritual truths woven together and presented on the platter of practical life applications. The life lessons you've shared have been painful but well worth it for the sake of others. I applaud your obedience. Coraleen, you were born to write. **--Pastor Terry Wayne Millender, Victorious Life Church**

I have known Coraleen almost ten years. She is a woman of integrity, great faith and love, with a strong commitment to God. She is a real prayer warrior and seeks the Lord with great passion. In her writing she gives you access to the things God has used in the past to bring her to Himself.

As the reader journeys with her, you will feel the pain, joy, hope, love, and other emotions of a young child as she walks through life's experiences. Her love of God's Word will be an encouragement as she uses it to teach life's principles.

I have watched Coraleen over these years as she has gone through many trials and struggles, always looking to God. She has grown and matured in a wonderful way.

God has given Coraleen some beautiful gifts that she has used to bless the Body of Christ. I am pleased to call her my friend.

-Reverend Alice Holland, Aglow International Prayer Coordinator of Washington, D.C. & Virginia

DEDICATION

To my siblings, Paulette, Sherry, and Fleetwood, whom I love with all my heart. My greatest desire and deepest prayer is to impact the Kingdom of God for His glory.

ACKNOWLEDGMENTS

To my daughters, Renee, Racquel, Lakisha and Nichelle, and my son-in law Malcolm: you are great and have been a blessing to me in many ways. I would not change any thing about you. You all are unique in your own way. I love you very much.

To Alex, Alice, Benjamin, Toni and Judy: thank you all for rendering your gift to this book. I love you a bunch! Special thanks to Kathie Nee Scriven, of Scriven Communications, for your editing and consulting services.

To Pat: you are my number one fan and I could not have achieved any of my accomplishments without your support. You have believed in me and that means so much to me. I love you very much!

To Pastor Decker and Delores: you just keep giving and giving. What a wonderful example of spiritual mentors, coaches, and confidants to imitate we have at Faith Christian Church and International Outreach Center.

To all my friends who have prayed for me while I was writing this book: your prayers helped me get through the writer's block syndrome. Don't stop! Thank you a million times over.

To Father: thank you for sharing Your heart with me. It is what I long for every day when I first open my eyes. To Jesus: I love You. I desire You. But, most of all, I need You every day of my life. To the Holy Spirit: thank You for Your ingenious creativity and being the mastermind of this project…showing me how to put this all together.

Eyes have not seen nor have ears heard…the things which God has prepared for me because I love Him. **(2 Corinthians 2:9)**

TABLE OF CONTENTS

FOREWORD

Living in a world that's changes like the wind with limited connection with God is frightening. Man has experimented in areas that make him feel as though he is God. In many areas in this world we have become ashamed to call on God's name publicly. However, with the uncertainties, disasters and the struggles that we are facing on a daily basis is causing mankind to pray. We are asking God to extend his grace upon mankind while we are lamenting over the ills of this world. But as time moves on, it dwindles down and allows individuals to go through and discover what grace is all about. Once you really experience God's grace and **KNOW** it is God's grace we can focus on Him.

According to man, grace is not fair, because he can't comprehend God's amazing grace in spiritual realm, therefore, leaving him physically perplexed. Grace is God's ability in you to move on or to hang in there, in spite of the circumstances **KNOWING** that God did not abandon you. You can't substitute your emotions or technology for your total submission to the will of God. The bible tells us, our ways are not His or our thoughts, therefore when it comes to grace it belongs to God. God is in control. Understanding this fact as truth may be a struggle for some, depending on your relationship with God.

As a believer you should be encouraged to rely on God's grace, because of His love that has been demonstrated towards you. If you reflect back over your life, you will run into a few situations that will come to your remembrance and remind you, if it had not been for God's grace, you may be sleeping in your grave. Thank God for grace! Now, for the unbelievers, you may be struggling trying to hold on, be encouraged you are about to see the light at the end of the tunnel, still it is God's grace upon your life.

Evangelist Coraleen F. Braxton has written this book to challenge your understanding about God's amazing grace. What's amazing about God's grace? You can function with joy, peace and love knowing that God will sustain you. Through her experiences she developed a stronger awareness of His grace.

Dr. Karyn C. Jones
Executive Vice President/Administration
Faith Christian University and Schools

INTRODUCTION

I did not write this book exclusively with the Church in mind. The Church is adequately supplied with books on prayer, self-help, leadership, and the glory of God, just to name a few. This book was written for those who are not in leadership positions, for those in the Church and not in the Church who are struggling with patterns of unhealthy behavior, and for those who are in a valley of decision and uncertain about which path of life to take.

People are searching for answers and wondering who will speak the truth and nothing but the truth. They want to know if there is someone who can relate to their present struggles, in addition to this, they want someone who can affirm that they are not a bad person, but simply an imperfect one, working out their own salvation with fear and trembling. **(Philippians 2:12)** If they continue in the process with the right mindsets, God will turn their hopelessness into bridges of hope. That is just the kind of God we serve!

This book is divided into two parts. In Part I will share: "What is Grace? Why Does Man Need Grace? Jesus' Mission, and Growing in Grace" along with other pertinent topics to increase the reader awareness of *Living in the Amazing Grace of God*. In Part II, I will share my testimony highlighting major parts of my life along with some life lessons.

I pray that this book will have an impact on your life, because after capturing and writing about all of my childhood, (and young-adult experiences), it was revealed to me, that not only was the hand of God, but also the grace of God was upon my life. I believe that the Lord had one thing on His mind in allowing me to go through the adversity I did "…**That I may know him, and the power of his resurrection, and the fellowship**

of his sufferings, being made conformable unto his death." (Philippians 3:10)

It is inconceivable to imagine that the Almighty God created me with a specific purpose to perform in this vast cosmos. I have experienced persecutions, abandonment, abuse, fatigue and heartaches. But there is no problem that is uncommon to man. Evil knows no boundaries, and it comes to destroy us all. God did not take me out of the storms of life, but He did protect me in them. If not for God's grace, I would have ended up in jail, suffering from some incurable disease, or six feet under the earth. **"But this one thing I know is that God favored and delighted in me, because He did not allow my enemy to triumph over me." (Psalm 41:11)**

Jesus told Peter that the devil wanted to separate him from his faith in God. God allowed the attack, but Jesus assured Peter that He had prayed especially for him. Once Peter was converted; he was qualified to strengthen his brothers. The purpose for sharing my memoir and experiences is to encourage my readers and let them know that you are not alone. If I came through, you can also come through if you keep focused on God and remain obedient to Him. God's grace is sufficient!

I am a visual person; therefore God showed me what *grace* looked like by giving me a vision. In the vision, I am walking along a path that I usually take every day. I am watching and praying, but somehow I stumble. It is evident by the way that my body is moving with gravity that I am about to land flat on my face. The next thing I know, I am walking upright again. Psalm 91:11-12 states, **"For He shall give his angels charge over thee, to keep thee in all thy ways. They shall bear thee up in their hands, lest thou dash thy foot against a stone."**

My question to the Lord was "Why did I stumble?" I believe that He showed me that at some point along the path, I stopped watching. The angels were ministering spirits sent to serve me, and to keep me from falling. **(Hebrews 1:14)**

I believe that another reason that we may stumble, at times, is because the devil sets snares. That is how he operates – with deceit, cunning and trickery. It does not mean that I have done anything wrong; it is just the devil's nature to try to cause me to fall. The majority of these snares were successful during my formative years, when I had no defense mechanism to fight back with, in order to ward off or to resist the attack.

A famous gospel songwriter recorded a song with the following lyrics, *"We fall down but we get up, for a saint is just a sinner who fell down, and got up."*

"Now unto him that is able to keep you from falling and to present you faultless before the presence of his glory with exceeding joy." (Jude 1:24)

All scriptures are taken from the King James Version© 2005 unless otherwise stated.

PART I

GROWING IN GRACE

What is Grace?

The biblical definition of grace is unmerited or undeserved favor, the goodness or special love of God. The Greek word for grace is translated as "*cha'ris, and when received by faith, transforms man and causes him to love and to seek after the righteousness of God"* **(Zodhiates, 1469).**[1]

2 Corinthians 5:17: "Therefore if any man be in Christ, he is a new creature: old things are passed away; behold all things are become new."

Grace changes us without destroying our personality. No personality is bad, but to work on developing weak areas of your personality will take the grace of God.

All humans born into the earth today are undeserving of and have lost all claims to God's grace because of Adam and Eve's sin against Him. However, due to God's mercy, which is His compassion and love for us, He provided a Savior, Jesus Christ, to reconcile us back to Himself. Mercy was God's motivating factor for extending His grace to us again. If the believer receives God's grace in faith, it will bring joy and produce a thankful heart.

2 Corinthians 5:18: "And all things are of God, who hath reconciled us to himself by Jesus Christ, and hath given to us the ministry of reconciliation…"

John 3:16: "For God so loved the world, that he gave his only begotten Son, that whosoever believeth in him should not perish, but have everlasting life."

1 John 4:9-10: "In this was manifested the love of God toward us, because God sent his only begotten Son into the world that we might live through him. Herein is love, not that we loved God, but that he loved us, and sent his Son to be the propitiation for our sins."

Why Does Man Need Grace?

When God created the first man, Adam, he was made into God's image and likeness. Adam possessed God's righteousness, holiness and knowledge.

Ephesians 4:24: "And that ye put on the new man, which after God is created in righteousness and true holiness."

Colossians 3:10: "And have put on the new man, which is renewed in knowledge after the image of him that created him:"

The creation of *man* was God's apex of His entire creation. He crowned man with both glory and honor. Man was to rule over all His works. In other words, God gave man ruler-ship and His delegated authority to rule in the earth. God also wanted to have fellowship with man. That union was broken when Adam and Eve sinned.

Psalm 8:5-6: "For thou hast made him a little lower than the angels, and hast crowned him with glory and honour. Thou madest him to have dominion over the works of thy hands; thou hast put all things under his feet..."

Hebrews 2:6-8: "What is man, that thou art mindful of him? Or the son of man, that thou visitest him? Thou madest him a little lower than the angels; thou crownedst him with glory and honour, and didst set him over the works of thy hands: Thou hast put all things in subjection under his feet. For in that he put all in subjection under him, he left nothing that is not put under him. But now we see not yet all things put under him.'"

Man needed grace when his ruler-ship was interrupted in the Garden of Eden. *"In the Fall, the soul refused the rule of the spirit and became the slave of the body with its appetites. Man became flesh, and the spirit lost its rule and became little more than a dormant power. It was no longer a ruling principle but a struggling captive. The spirit now stands in opposition to the flesh (the word for the life of the soul and the body together) in its subjection to sin"* **(Murray, 24).**[2]

God gave Adam specific instructions to eat from any tree in the garden except the tree of knowledge of good and evil; this was to avoid death.

Genesis 1:29: "And God said, Behold, I have given you every herb bearing seed, which is upon the face of all the earth, and every tree, in the which is the fruit of a tree yielding seed; to you it shall be for meat."

Genesis 2:8-9: "And the Lord God planted a garden eastward in Eden; and there he put the man whom he had formed. And out of the ground made the Lord God to grow every tree that is pleasant to the sight, and good for food; the tree of life also in the midst of the garden, and the tree of knowledge of good and evil."

Genesis 2:16: "And the Lord God commanded the man, saying, 'of every tree of the garden thou mayest freely eat:'"

The serpent and deceiver (which was one of God's creatures), approached Eve whom God had created to be Adam's helpmeet. *"The question whether it was sin or not to eat of this tree, and whether really the fruit of it was forbidden"* **(Henry, 8).**[3] Eve already knew the answer was affirmative to the question, but, the enemy put doubt into her mind to question God's motive for His instruction.

Genesis 3:1: "Now the serpent was more subtle than any beast of the field which the Lord God had made. And he said unto the woman, 'Yea, hath God said, Ye shall not eat of every tree of the garden?' "

Genesis 3:3-5: "But of the fruit of the tree which is in the midst of the garden, God hath said, Ye shall not eat of it, neither shall ye touch it, lest ye die. And the

serpent said unto the woman, Ye shall not surely die: For God doth know that in the day ye eat thereof, then your eyes shall be opened, and ye shall be as gods, knowing good and evil."

Therefore, Eve was deceived into believing the enemy and responded contrary to the will of God and ate the forbidden fruit. Eve then gave to Adam and he ate also, thus man lost his position and authority in the earth because he sinned against God.

Genesis 3:6: "And when the woman saw that the tree was good for food, and that it was pleasant to the eyes, and a tree to be desired to make one wise, she took of the fruit thereof, and did eat, and gave also unto her husband with her; and he did eat."

Now that Adam had committed high-treason against the kingdom of God, he could no longer dwell in the presence of God. God cursed the serpent but He judged Adam and Eve for the sin they committed.

Though Adam and Eve suffered the consequences for their disobedience, God extended mercy and provided sufficient clothing to cover their shame which was an act of grace. But the ultimate consequence remained - man was separated from the presence of God.

Genesis 3:21-23: "Unto Adam also and to his wife did the Lord God make coats of skins, and clothed them. And the Lord God said, Behold, the man is become as one of us, to know good and evil: and now, lest he put forth his hand, and take also of the tree of life, and eat, and live for ever: Therefore the Lord God sent him forth from the garden of Eden, to till the ground from whence he was taken."

Jesus' Mission

Now that humanity had fallen from grace, Jesus' coming and subsequent death to redeem mankind was necessary. Humanity needed a Savior and Jesus was the atoning sacrifice or man's sin.

Man was lost in his sin and had no way back to the Father's grace. Man had ceased being a living spirit and now was a dead soul. Jesus made it possible for us to have the eternal life we once lost.

It was the Father's will that we be made holy and brought into fellowship with Him again. Jesus' sacrificial death on the cross justified all those who believe and accept what He did to embrace the Father's grace.

Galatians 5:4: "Christ is become of no effect unto you, whosoever of you are justified by the law; ye are fallen from grace."

John 10:10: "The thief cometh not, but for to steal, and to kill, and to destroy: I am come that they might have life, and that they might have it more abundantly."

Hebrews 10:9-10: "Then said he, Lo, I come to do thy will, O God. He taketh away the first, that he may establish the second. By the which will we are sanctified through the offering of the body of Jesus Christ once for all."

Jesus' Ministry was to Save, Heal, and Deliver

The ministry of Jesus is recorded in both the Old and New Testament. As a matter of fact there are countless scriptures in the Bible where Jesus healed the sick, raised the dead and both opened blind eyes and deaf ears. The Apostle John wrote that despite everything written in the gospels about Jesus' ministry, there were still countless other acts that went unrecorded.

John 21:25: "And there are also many other things which Jesus did, the which, if they should be written every one, I suppose that even the world itself could not contain the books that should be written. Amen."

Isaiah chapter 61 and Luke chapter 4 record the ministry of Jesus almost verbatim. In the above chapter, Isaiah prophesied about the year of the Lord's favor concerning the coming Messiah who would have a ministry of restoration and would proclaim good tidings to the poor and needy. Luke records right around the time A.D. 60, that Jesus picked up the scroll of the prophet Isaiah and read what Isaiah proclaimed about His ministry.

Jesus was anointed to meet the needs of humanity. He also preached the good news of the kingdom (God's way of doing things). Jesus' ministry was very effective and the crowds were amazed because He taught with authority.

Therefore, those who believed and received the words of Jesus by faith, benefited from His ministry. Jesus came to heal the sick, deliver those who were oppressed by the enemy and call the sinners to repentance.

Luke 4:17-19: "And there was delivered unto him the book of the prophet Esaias. And when he had opened the book, he found the place where it was written, the Spirit of the Lord is upon me, because he hath

anointed me to preach the gospel to the poor; he hath sent me to heal the brokenhearted, to preach deliverance to the captives, and recovering of sight to the blind, to set at liberty them that are bruised, to preach the acceptable year of the Lord."

Matthew 7:28-29: "And it came to pass, when Jesus had ended these sayings, the people were astonished at his doctrine: For he taught them as one having authority, and not as the scribes."

Luke 5:31-32: "And Jesus answering said unto them, they that are whole need not a physician; but they that are sick. I came not to call the righteous, but sinners to repentance."

Growing in Grace

In his epistle, Peter instructs us as follows: **"But grow in grace and in the knowledge of our Lord and Saviour Jesus Christ. To him be glory both now and for ever. Amen." (2 Peter 3:18)**

The Greek word for grow is aulo's and translated, *"to give increase, cause to grow, to exceed and enlarge"* **(289).**1

Growing in the grace of God is contingent on the individual believer knowing that they possess God's grace. You can read about God's favor on your life and people can tell you that God favors you, but you have to believe it to know that you are continually *Living in the grace of God*. Know grace is real whether you are going through bad times, indifferent times or just trying to grow in your Christian walk. This determines the life you live and the results you get. Again, it's like the analogy of visualizing the glass half empty or half full.

Therefore, in order to believe and grow in the grace of God you have to know for yourself that you have sufficient grace, regardless of your bitter-sweet journey to an overcoming life.

James 2: 14, 20, 26: "Dear friends, do you think you'll get anywhere in this if you learn all the right words but never do anything? Does merely talking about faith indicate that a person really has it...Isn't it obvious that God-talk without God-acts is outrageous nonsense? ...Separate faith and works and you get the same thing: a corpse." (Message Bible)

If we are believers in Jesus and we imitate His lifestyle, we have the same grace that He had upon His life from the Father. The Bible declares that Jesus was a man who experienced a bitter-sweet journey (rejection, scorn, suffering and sorrow), however, God's grace was sufficient for Him to overcome in His afflictions and to complete His earthly assignment in love. Grace doesn't change or destroy the believer's individuality, but it causes the believer to love more while pressing towards the high calling in Christ Jesus.

The Divine Process of Grace

As we continue to grow in grace, it causes us to increase in our love towards one another, can help us to experience joy in times of sorrow, peace when we become perplexed about a situation and receive other blessings in our time of desperate need.

I believe as we walk through our trials (which are often described as dark times in our life), God gives us special revelation about His goodness to encourage our faith. The Bible states that Joseph and the Israelites were prosperous in their time of affliction.

Genesis 41:52: "And the name of the second called he Ephraim: For God hath caused me to be fruitful in the land of my affliction."

Exodus 1:12: "But the more they afflicted them, the more they multiplied and grew. And they were grieved because of the children of Israel."

Here are a few more examples of biblical characters who received special grace and revelation during times of testing and trial: The Apostle John was dragged from Ephesus in chains and exiled to the Isle of Patmos where he received revelation about Jesus Christ. Jesus appeared to John in his isolation and revealed the future to him that would affect generations to come.

Jacob received revelation when he saw God face-to-face in a dark time or hour of his life when he was in a very difficult situation. An angry father-in-law manipulated and cheated him which provoked Jacob to reciprocate the sin. When Jacob asked for Rachel's hand in marriage, he had to work for Laban (his father-in-law) for seven years. When the time was complete, Laban deceived Jacob and gave Leah because it was customary to give the firstborn in marriage first.

Jacob's hostile and embittered brother, Esau, planned to kill Jacob for stealing his birthright. Jacob deceived his father on his death bed to bless him with the blessing of the firstborn which legally belonged to Esau.

Jacob's life was now coming full circle and he was alone by the Jabbok, where he wrestled with a man (angel) until daybreak. When the man saw that he could not overpower Jacob, he touched the socket of Jacob's hip. In the conformation, Jacob was given the revelation that he was struggling with God and with men and had overcome. Jacob's name was also changed to Israel and his life was spared from Laban and Esau.

Last but not least, there was Job who was at his lowest point when he lost everything in one day! He was stricken with grief and agonizing pain as he questioned God about his situation.

Starting in chapter 40 of the book of Job, he gets a revelation of Almighty God who appeared to Job in a whirlwind and spoke to him about the mysteries of God. The experience was so life-changing to Job that in Job chapter 42 verses 2-5 he states: **"I know that thou canst do every thing, and that no thought can be withholden from thee. Who is he that hideth counsel without knowledge? Therefore have I uttered that I understood not; things too wonderful for me, which I knew not. Hear, I beseech thee, and I will speak: I will demand of thee, and declare thou unto me. I have heard of thee by the hearing of the ear: but now mine eye seeth thee."**

I am convinced that God wants to give us a revelation of Himself in our dark hours. One of the reasons for this I believe is that we can comfort others with the comfort He has given us. He wants us to be givers of His grace to help comfort others who are going through tough times.

Ephesians 4:7: "But unto every one of us is given grace according to the measure of the gift of Christ."

Philippians 1:7: "Even as it is meet for me to think this of you all, because I have you in my heart;

inasmuch as both in my bonds, and in the defense and confirmation of the gospel, ye all are partakers of my grace."

I believe it would be difficult for me to intercede for others or empathize or sympathize with their pain if I have not experienced pain, grief and sufferings myself.

I am not suggesting that we should have a *Messiah's complex,* but as Jesus was touched with our infirmities – "so is He, so are we!" Jesus is our High Priest and we have been called as priests and kings in the kingdom of God.

Hebrews 4:15: "For we have not an high priest which cannot be touched with the feeling of our infirmities; but was in all points tempted like as we are, yet without sin."

1 John 4:17: "Herein is our love made perfect, that we may have boldness in the day of judgment: because as he is, so are we in this world."

Revelations 1:6: "And hath made us kings and priests unto God and his Father; to him be glory and dominion for ever and ever. Amen."

We have obtained this grace to help lift the spirits of others and we are empowered to do so because the grace of God opens up a new world of abundant blessings and inexpressible joy when we press through trials with the right attitude.

The right attitude will cause us to overcome in the trial versus the bad attitude will cause us to be subdued by the trial. I am reminded of **Deuteronomy 30:19, "I call heaven and earth to record this day against you, that I have set before you life and death, blessing and cursing: therefore choose life that both thou and thy seed may live."**

As long as we have an enemy, spiritual warfare is not going to go away, we just need to learn to fight the good fight of faith!

Psalm 30:5: "For his anger endureth but a moment; in his favour is life: weeping may endure for a night, but joy cometh in the morning."

The Physical Growth Process

There must be some element of life in a person or organism to cause growth. Death cannot produce life but God's breath of life can cause dead things to live! In other words, life only produces life.

Genesis 1:11: "And God said, 'Let the earth bring forth grass, the herb yielding seed, and the fruit tree yielding fruit after his kind, whose seed is in itself, upon the earth: and it was so.'"

Ezekiel 37:4-5: "Again he said unto me, Prophesy upon these bones, and say unto them, O ye dry bones, hear the word of the Lord. Thus saith the Lord God unto these bones; Behold, I will cause breath to enter into you, and ye shall live..."

Before a baby is born into the earth, the baby lives inside the pregnant mother's womb. The baby lives from the substances that are received from the mother's daily dietary intake. If the mother's daily dietary intake is hindered or unhealthy for a length of time, for any reason the risk of the baby becoming brain damaged or otherwise deformed or even experiencing death is increased.

On the other hand, if the pregnant mother's daily dietary intake contains all of the basic food groups and she has not formerly abused her health, the chances of the baby being born healthy are increased.

I do realize that there are unforeseen reasons in which a baby can be deformed or have other complications at birth. My purpose is to illustrate how the natural physical growing process parallels with the divine process of growing in grace.

The Infant Stage

When we are born into the Kingdom of God by the grace of God we are baby Christians. We often feel helpless at this stage but it seems as if every prayer we pray is answered by God - and in a speedy manner. There is no waiting!

Galatians 1:15: "But when it pleased God, who separated me from my mother's womb, and called me by his grace…"

When we are infants in the natural, we have everything done for us. We need to be fed, bathed and clothed. We need a grace-giver so to speak!

Life is usually smooth sailing because when the infant cries, the helping hands of the parents or guardians are there to meet every need. The child is the recipient of grace and does not understand anything about being a grace-giver. Even as a toddler the child is still oblivious about grace. The term, the "*terrible two's*" suggest that it's all about the child and no one else.

The Adolescent Stage

When we are adolescents, we are growing in the grace of God and these are difficult moments for us because our hormones are developing and emotions are running wild.

This is the stage where we are trying to fit in with the crowd and be accepted. Adolescents don't want to be identified with their parents because of the difference in their parents' age and their thinking. They choose to identify instead with their peers.

These are also difficult times because if at this stage the teenagers did not obey their parents in past years, they are usually now evermore so rebellious and defiant to authority. They still don't have any concept about giving grace but they certainly usually want abundant grace when they disobey.

This may not apply to all adolescents because there are some that are well-behaved. However, this is the stage where adolescents experience many growing pains and need much grace.

2 Peter 1:2: "Grace and peace be multiplied unto you through the knowledge of God, and of Jesus our Lord..."

Later in this discourse, you will read about some of my difficult moments and how those experiences affected my emotional and spiritual growth.

The Middle-Age Years

Once we have come through the school of *hard-knocks* and prayerfully developed into responsible adults, we should experience the reciprocal nature of grace: whatsoever a person sows, he will reap!

My former middle-age years awakened me to the fact that I was living in the amazing grace of God – even though I was on my bitter-sweet journey in life and having no real impact. I felt fairly content with my life at that time because I had a good job, home, family, car and money in the bank. I was blessed but I did not realize that I was blessed to be a blessing.

As a believer, my desire was to be used by God but my attitude was "please leave me alone and I will leave you alone!" Thus, the threat of perplexing experiences I encountered made it seem as if my life was invaded with all types of trouble. These encounters revealed what was in my heart and that I was selfish. They were to bring out the best in me. Now that I understand that I was being processed, my desire to be used by God would be fulfilled.

I experienced moments of triumph living in the amazing grace of God during this time period because I experienced victory at times, but not without a cost. My experiences in the middle-age years were challenging but they definitely offered me new opportunities for spiritual growth.

In this stage of my life I learned to give grace as much as receive grace because it is the heart of God, and I wanted His heartbeat. I was changing…evolving into something beautiful!

2 Corinthians 4:7: "But we have this treasure in earthen vessels, that the excellency of the power may be of God, and not of us."

The Retirement and Later Years

These are the golden years. Hopefully you have learned some valuable lessons along your path of life and are apt to teach the younger generation. You are walking in the grace of God and you have matured and you are hopefully living a fruitful life.

You understand what grace is, and you give it freely even if it is not extended to you in return. Oh, you still have some trials and tests but you expect them and you know how to count them all joy. There is less of you and more of Christ in you being revealed to the world. You have found the real secret to life: if you lose your (self) life – you will gain (Christ) life more abundantly.

Matthew 10:39: "He that findeth his life shall lose it: and he that loseth his life for my sake shall find it."

Galatians 2:20: "I am crucified with Christ: nevertheless I live; yet not I, but Christ liveth in me: and the life which I now live in the flesh I live by the faith of the Son of God, who loved me, and gave himself for me."

Part II

TESTIMONY

A Bitter-Sweet Journey to an Overcoming Life

Once Rejected but now Accepted

"To the praise of the glory of His grace, which He freely bestowed on us in the Beloved." (Ephesians 1:6) NASB

I was an unhappy, fat child in grade school - unhappy because of the cruel fiery darts that my peers thrust at me, and tilting the scale at 206 pounds by junior high school. I encountered rejection constantly. The denigrating remarks from the neighborhood boys, such as valley dale pig (the term was taken from a television commercial advertising bacon) and loud shouts of "look who wears short shorts". This was a joke that the neighborhood boys picked up when they saw me wear shorts for the first time. They said that I had a pretty face. The last remark was clearly implied and crippled me…, "you have a pretty face but an ugly body."

The repulsive looks from the girls, as if I was less virtuous than they were, was also a heavy load I had to bear. I was miserable and people added to my suffering. You could say I was looking for love, acceptance and approval. Food became my greatest pleasure, so it became a vicious cycle. The death sentence from my peers left me a coward, living a pretty solitary life.

By looking at me, you could see I had issues. However other people's problems were not as visible because they were camouflaged. Therefore, I was the brunt of people's jokes to hide their own gross insufficiencies.

When I was in junior high school, a classmate of mine, named Deborah Burke was very pretty and had so many clothes; she seemed to wear a different outfit every day. She lived with her grandmother who sold liquor illegally in her house. Her mom was an alcoholic and a drug addict and I cannot recall much about her father. I just know she did not live with them. Deborah became my friend and she was very nice to me. She talked to me and did not shun me. It was nice to be around her and see all the gorgeous outfits she wore.

Deborah did not have many friends either because all the girls were jealous of her beauty and style. Maybe the reason Deborah and I got along so well is because we both were starving for acceptance. I don't know where Deborah is now, but I pray that she is a Christian and her relationship with her mother and father is restored. And thanks, Deborah, (if you are out there) for being my friend and not rejecting me.

When I think back to an incident in class one day, the grace of God was surely upon my life. I was sharpening my pencil before class began. I am not sure where the teacher was but the class was unsupervised. There was a boy named Wayne and he was teasing me. I tried extremely hard to ignore his verbal abuse.

Soon the other boys began to join in on this verbal attack. I could feel the anger rising up in me and the tears rushing to the surface of my eyelids. The anger was an accumulation of all the past malicious persecutions I received. I cannot recollect all my thoughts at the time but from my reaction, I know, they were not godly. Wayne sputtered out a derogatory remark about my mother. Well, the boiling pot was ready and Wayne received the wrath of it.

The pencil that I was sharpening was finally sharp and it became the weapon I used for attempted murder. However, instead of it going into the side of his forehead where I was aiming, Wayne caught the lead in his hand when he tried to block me. I did not end up in jail but I had to write a statement describing the occurrence. I cannot think of any more rejection encountered that school year. I heard someone say that all it takes to teach a lesson to bullies is to have one of them become a sacrificial lamb.

However, as an adult, God eventually delivered me from a murdering spirit. I can understand the mind of the troubled minor who has been teased all his or her life and one day goes on a killing spree. I certainly don't recommend this type behavior, because I have been there. Insanity brings negative consequences!

I observed as the years went on that many of those who bullied me so badly seemed to reap their own negative consequences. One young man died an early death from obesity. His brother was also shot down cold-blooded. Many others are strung out on drugs to this day. I don't rejoice over their misfortunes in life, because they were struggling with their own dysfunctions. They were just blinded by the fact that once the devil is through employing you to cripple others, you will reap what you sow.

However, this one thing I know that God is pleased with me, because He did not let my enemy to triumph over me. He preserved my life because I was innocent; He has brought me into His presence forever. **(Psalm 41:11-12)**

Set Apart

"And while they were ministering to the Lord and fasting, the Holy Spirit said, 'Set apart for Me Barnabas and Saul for the work to which I have called them.' " (Acts 13:2) NASB

God's desire for every believer is that we should be sanctified. **(1 Thessalonians 4:3)** God wants to take the common and make it holy. We were designed to be holy because the mandate given by God to us is **"Be holy, because I am holy." (1 Peter 1:16)** Holiness is a significant characteristic of God; therefore, holiness must characterize the believer.

To be holy or sanctified is a process that only the Holy Spirit can accomplish as we yield to Him. The process of sanctification is the gracious purpose of God to accomplish a work, for example, **Acts 13:2** states, **"As they ministered to the Lord, and fasted, the Holy Spirit said, 'Separate me Barnabas and Saul for the work unto which I have called them.' "** God has a call on each of our lives. It is impossible for a believer to live like the world and be blessed and successfully complete the assignment that God has for them.

I grew up in the city of Norfolk, Virginia, in a large, two-level house with my parents, one of my older sisters and a nerd younger brother. One of the attractions in our home was a beautiful china cabinet with oak wood trim and a glass enclosure. In this antique china cabinet were various ornaments and beautiful dishes that had intrinsic value to Momma-dear (a term of endearment that was given to my mother). Therefore, I was always inquisitive and drawn to the colors, shapes, and designs of these valuable ornaments, to investigate their beauty.

As a child, I often wondered why we never used the pretty dishes every day. Only on special occasions would we decorate the dining room table with the beautiful china and special silverware. Everything seemed to sparkle and give the room an atmosphere of elegance.

One holiday as we were cleaning up the dishes and carefully putting them back on display in the china cabinet, I asked Momma-dear, "Why don't we use these dishes every day? They are so pretty!" Momma-dear exclaimed, "These are special dishes that we only use for special occasions, for special guests. If we use them every day we may break them. They are hard to replace because they came from overseas. That's why we set them apart to protect them." This wonderful memory is symbolic of sanctification.

The word *sanctification* in Greek is *hagiazo*, and means to separate, set apart, purify, consecrate or to make holy. Anyone or anything that is dedicated to the Lord belongs to God to be used for His glory. **Numbers 6:1-2, 8** states, **"Again the Lord spoke to Moses, saying, 'Speak to the sons of Israel, and say to them, When a man or woman makes a special vow, the vow of a Nazarite, to dedicate himself to the Lord'...All the days of his separation he is holy to the Lord."** This is the same requirement for the modern day Christian. We must learn how to be set apart or sanctified from the world.

We must constantly remind ourselves to render our soul (intellect, will and emotions) over to the lordship of Jesus. We cannot think with a humanistic mindset and live a successful Christian life. Our wills must be examined daily to see if they are God honoring, and we must not allow our emotions to lead us.

Just as china is made to be used primarily just for special occasions, conversely, pottery is used on a daily basis. The difference is the purpose that the china and the pottery are designed for. Each believer is an exquisite piece of art, designed by God primarily for the purpose of good works. God knows our gifts, abilities and personality and how we fit into the scheme of His plans. John the Baptist would not have functioned well in the king's palace when he was designed to preach in the wilderness. Regardless, the inward cleansing, or purification, in a believer's life is the work of the Holy Spirit unto good works.

A Sanctified life is a self-surrendered and self-sacrificed life unto Christ. We don't live unto ourselves anymore, but Christ lives His life through us to benefit others. The process of sanctification may seem harsh to us at times because crucifixion is never a pleasant experience, but the rewards are great.

One of the key rewards is that we will eventually love others as Jesus loves. We will achieve this as we continue to yield our mind, emotions and will to His lordship. This is a great challenge because many believers are hurt and wounded from their past. Therefore, the tendency is to nurse those hurts and wounds. Our role is "to let go and let God," and sanctification will take place. The Holy Spirit will only do the will of the Father and the Scriptures declare that it is God's will for us to be wholly sanctified to Him. **"Now may the God of peace Himself sanctify you entirely; and may your spirit and soul and body be preserved complete, without blame at the coming of our Lord Jesus Christ." (1 Thessalonians 5:23)**

A Fit of Carnality

"...For the mind set on the flesh is death, but the mind set on the Spirit is life and peace." (Romans 8:6)

When I was a child, I was severely rejected because of my obesity, which left a sore spot in my life that never seemed to heal. Every time that spot was touched, shock waves would radiate through my body and send signals to my brain. I would become intoxicated with this unbearable pain and eventually sink into a miry pit. Thus, the journey began, and my mind was cloudy with negative thoughts. The cloud resembled smoke being puffed from a cigarette. It filled the atmosphere of my brain which caused every thought to reek with the smell of distortion.

I did not like being alone during these episodes, so I would call all my loyal housemates of my carnal mind. As the saying goes "misery loves company." They never failed to show up for a polluted party – these included: Self-Pity-Wallow, Insecurity, and Unforgiveness who always stoked the fire with fuel. Kingpin Rejection also usually strolled in late because he thought he was never invited to any of these polluted events. He felt uncomfortable arriving alone so he was accompanied by his twin cousins, Fear of Rejection and Self-Rejection Backup. Whatever support I needed, they contributed freely. Sometimes they would give more discouragement than I could handle.

Fortunately I had one godly friend, named Positive Antidote. During many of these fits, Positive Antidote made every effort to encourage me to come out of my miserable condition. He was refreshing and quite helpful, if I heeded His counsel. However, if my ungodly friends had spent any length of time with me in this drunken stupor, it seemed like a losing battle. Positive Antidote was hated by his opponents because He was always encouraging me with the truth to counteract the lies and deception of the carnal mind.

Whenever Positive Antidote appeared, Kingpin Rejection would incite his twin cousin to keep me consumed in my own little world...and I would reject any counsel from Positive Antidote. However, Positive Antidote was always interceding on my behalf. As seconds, hours and occasionally days lapsed, I would be flooded with light and eventually come out of my fit of carnality.

This is an illustration of what transpires in the carnal mind if you or I allow it to take over. You can't allow negative thoughts to come to you mind – however, you (your spirit man) can make a decision through your will to keep from dwelling on them. By dwelling on them, you are sowing to the flesh. **"For the one who sows to his own flesh shall from the flesh reap corruption, but the one who sows to the Spirit shall from the Spirit reap eternal life." (Galatians 6:8)**

We are told to cast out every imagination that exalts itself against the knowledge of God. **"Casting down imaginations, and every high thing that exalteth itself against the knowledge of God, and bringing into captivity every thought to the obedience of Christ." (2 Corinthians 10:5)** The key is to keep from dwelling on these thoughts and to replace them with the word of God.

If I get offended and become ensnared by the enemy, because of the day to day things that people say or do to me, then I am then essentially still holding onto my past. One of the devil's major weapons is the spirit of offense. **Luke 17:1, "Then said he unto the disciples, it is impossible but that offences will come: but woe unto him, through whom they come!"** On the same token, I could be the one to offend another, whether intentionally or unintentionally by my actions or words. As a matter of fact, I am certain the devil has presented you and I with the temptation to receive and give offense today. The Bible says there is no temptation that is uncommon to any of us. **1 Corinthians 10:13** says, **"No temptation has overtaken you but such as is common to man; and God is faithful, who will not allow you to be tempted beyond what you are able, but with the temptation will provide the way of escape also, that you may be able to endure it."**

Some of the great men of God were tempted with the spirit of offense, men such as Jeremiah, Elijah, and even John the Baptist. They were men with like passions. The good thing about any temptation is that God has provided a way in which we do not have to yield to it.

I have learned through the years that it is wise to *respond* and not to *react* to the temptation. When we respond to a difficult situation it is by the Spirit, but when we react it is normally through the flesh. **James 4:7** counsels us to **"Submit therefore to God. Resist the devil and he will flee from you."** I may feel like lashing back with mean words, or pouting or mentally dwelling on how much someone hurt me by what they said. I have not totally arrived, but I am learning to master my emotions and not let my emotions master me. If this area of being controlled by your emotions has been a pattern of your life for a while or if it's been a stronghold in your life for a long time, realize that you may not be miraculously delivered from this behavior overnight. But once we recognize that it is sin and make it a matter of prayer to improve, we should see results fairly quickly. We are told to just press on!

I have to be aware because the devil does not play fair. He will take full advantage of any situation if I give in to his ways. I refuse to allow him to cause me to sink into a fit of carnality any longer.

We all have hurtful pasts, but when Jesus arrived on the scene, that should be the end of our past…period. My spirit is reborn and I must renew my soul/mind (which includes my thoughts, will and emotions). **"Therefore if any man is in Christ, he is a new creature; the old things passed away; behold, new things have come." (2 Corinthians 5:17)** Let us not get in agreement and fellowship with the carnal mind. If we sow to the flesh, we will reap death, but if we sow to the Spirit we shall reap eternal life which is our inheritance.

"Finally, brethren, whatever is true, whatever is honorable, whatever is right, whatever is pure, whatever is lovely, whatever is of good repute, if there is any excellence and if anything worthy of praise, let your mind dwell on these things." (Philippians 4:8)

Exposed by Grace

"And he said unto me, My grace is sufficient for thee: for my strength is made perfect in weakness. Most gladly therefore will I rather glory in my infirmities, that the power of Christ may rest upon me." (2 Corinthians 12:9)

After the death of my first husband who died from cancer two years after we were married, I remarried at the age of 23. My second husband was in the military and our marriage began to go sour six months after our union. However, I am from the old school: stay married until death.

In the summer of 1985 my husband received a permanent change of station orders to live in Germany for four years. I was undecided about going with him because my marriage was steadily deteriorating, but I was convinced by many people that I should not let him go to Germany alone. Reluctantly, I agreed and for the next six months we prepared to move that September with our three daughters who were 12, 7 and 3 at the time.

I am very mentally affected by climate changes. I enjoy warm weather, sunshine and being outdoors and it is very therapeutic. The climate change was very noticeable to me when we arrived in Europe. There was a heavy cloud that hovered over the country. I could see it and I could feel it; I did not like it.

I had never experienced depression before, but now (20 years later) looking back on my destructive behavior, my spirit had sunk to a new low. To add to my depressed condition, it took a couple of months for me to get employed again by a government agency. Therefore, I camouflaged all my pain by jogging, and began to secretly engage in the eating disorder anorexia/bulimia.

A month after we arrived in Germany my husband and I attended a company commander's social function to be formally introduced to the people in the company. I thought that the function was quite boring. It appeared that the wives of these military husbands did not have real meaning to their lives. It seemed that most of them were desperate wives living in their husband's shadow.

Any time I was approached by one of them, the conversation always started out with "Hi, my name is…. 'What do you do?" If I did not say what I wanted to say in that breath my chance to add anything else was over.

Then they would proceed to talk about their *big man on campus*. I would put on a happy face, as if I cared, while feeling like a hypocrite inside. I dreaded going to these functions. I knew my husband could tell because he could see it on my face: however, I would stomach it and suppress the resentment. I resented my husband and myself for moving to this foreign country and putting my career on hold while furthering his.

Every quarter we attended one of these social functions, and as usual, other new people were being formally introduced and welcomed. The African American couples in the company could be counted on one hand, and tonight one of the African American captain's fiancée (Joan) was being added to this social group. All of the women (including myself) huddled around Joan to engage her in polite discourse. I was a bit on the shy side, so I did a lot of observing. It was difficult for me to be happy for anyone coming into the company when I did not want to be there myself.

Well, we did not have to initiate any social politeness with Joan. Joan was different. As a matter of fact, there was no guile in her and she was outspoken. What really interested me about Joan was her candidness. She had an *in-your-face* type of personality. She began to say who she was and what she did. She was quite refreshing! She began to talk about the book she was writing. I cannot remember what it was about, because that was not what caught my attention in her discourse. It was her admission that she currently struggled with anorexia that interested me.

Let me digress at this point. I would have paid someone to take pictures of all the expressions on the women's faces when she first revealed that she was currently struggling with anorexia. Their eyes begin to widen and their mouths dropped open. I could sense by the expressions on many of the wives' faces that they felt uncomfortable with conversation of such intimate nature, seeing that they were only used to discussing superficial things. It also made me feel a little uncomfortable, but it was what I *needed* to hear even if it wasn't what I *wanted* to hear.

Even though Joan was struggling with anorexia in her recovery stage, I sense that she was rediscovering her identity and she was not afraid to say what was on her mind.

Joan continued to describe some of her distorted behavior associated with this eating disorder. She said she would carry a scale every place she went (and I mean on a day-to-day basis!). For example, if she was in the bank waiting in line, she would actually pull out the scale and weigh herself, over and again until she reached the teller to be served!

Soon the large huddle dwindled down until it was just Joan and I. I was not taken by surprise because I too struggled with anorexia and bulimia. As she continued to peak my interest, I can remember thinking, "I'm not that bad."

During the course of our tour in Germany, I never confessed to Joan that I was struggling with this eating disorder. I can only think of one reason why I did not share my struggle with Joan: the embarrassment of exposing my struggle to my husband and daughters. But, God used Joan to expose to me my self-destructive lifestyle, but I continued to live in denial for the next five years.

I was slowly killing myself. I was on a pendulum. I would starve myself one day, and the next day I would binge on food and then vomit because I felt guilty for eating. It took me a long time to share my problem with anyone, and especially with Christians, because I was living in guilt and shame. I was an expert at covering up any guilt and shame in my Christian life. I would buy the finest clothes to wear, fix my hair, use all the religious phrases and put on a happy face. But, my inner man was in constant turmoil because of my secret life.

When I finally confessed this eating disorder to some Christian friends, the responses varied. One Christian pastor was totally ignorant of the disorder – "never heard of it" was his response. Another pastor counseled me with instructions to speak positive words and think godly thoughts until the bad behavior ceased. Needless to say, I did this because I believed it, but the bad behavior seemed to get worse.

I eventually found a counselor who helped me understand the issues beneath the surface that I had camouflaged. I was very angry because of some of the blows that life had dealt me. Why did I have to be obese? I was afraid of becoming obese again. Why were people rejecting me?

Eating was my way of masking the problem of rejection, but I would eat too much and feel guilty and then purge all of the food that I had just consumed. It is no different than a drug addict or an alcoholic. Whatever we can find to dull the pain in our heart, we will reach for it. However, when the effects of the food, drug or alcohol wears off, the pain remains.

Why was I was raped by a man who I thought was my friend? I was in my early 20's and attending college with this man. We had known each other for two years before this incident occurred. We were like brother and sister.

He was living with his girlfriend at the time and she had just given birth to their new baby. She and the baby would be arriving home in a couple of days.

My attacker asked me if I would come and help him prepare the baby room and clean the house for their arrival. I was excited about their new baby and thought it was a nice gesture to help him. I had no reason to answer negatively.

My friend picked me up in his truck. We talked during the ride to his house about the new baby, and he expressed what he wanted to do in the future for his girlfriend and their new baby.

When we arrived at his house, I asked him which room he wanted me to start in first. He avoided my question and pretended as if he did not hear me, while walking into his bedroom. I followed him into the bedroom to question him again.

Once I entered into the bedroom, his conversation became offensive and his mannerism towards me became aggressive. By this time I knew he had more on his mind than cleaning. I tried to talk him out of his plan to rape me until I had to fight him. He was a body-builder and very muscular and he over-powered me.

When the rape was over I was angry, in shock, speechless and appalled that someone I considered a brother would hurt me in this way.

When I eventually got up the courage to confront my attacker, his response was, "You know you wanted it." I resented the fact that he insinuated it was my fault? This was an accusation that was imbedded deep in my soul. Therefore, for once I was going to be in control of my body. No one was going to hurt me again (was my thought). I did not realize that my own irresponsibility and humanistic thinking was just a form of self-rejection.

From then on, I rejected all my desires, dreams and visions. I spent all my energy trying to be someone that I was never meant to be and still ended up being frustrated. I did not say so with words, but my actions were telling God "I do not like the way you made me, and 'why did you make me this way?' " Boy, I sounded just like a private trying to give orders to the Commander-in-Chief. Sheer ignorance!

Also, as I was growing up as a child, I hated being black and would daydream of being white. At that time television and the culture were portraying that *blonds have more fun*, and I did not see any blue eyed, blond-haired black people having fun.

I never thought that I measured up to people's expectations and I was always trying to improve my looks. I wanted to look and be like other women who seemed, to me, to have it all together. They seemed to be popular and outgoing. Simply put…I did not love the woman God had created me to be.

My recollection is that most of the women suffering from anorexia in the 80's were Caucasians. They looked emaciated, and you could see the spirit of suicide and death upon their life. It was upon my life as well, but it was not noticeable in my appearance. In my ignorance and self-will, God's grace protected me from self-destructing.

My recovery began when I first started seeing this particular counselor I had found through my health care provider, but, it was a slow progress.

The counseling allowed me to get in touch with buried hurts, wounds and fragile emotions. I had good days, weeks, and eventually months without having any episodes until I was totally free from anorexia and bulimia. I am grateful to Joan's honesty and her *in-your-face* personality because I was *Exposed by Grace.*

Father Knows Best

"The Lord will perfect that which concerns me..." (Psalm 138:8)

It was 1995; I had been separated and divorced for five years. As I stated previously, my marriage was on shaky ground six months after my husband and I got married. He would leave the house on the week-end and go stay with his girlfriend and then return home on Monday after his workday. One day he came home from work and packed his clothes and left me and the children. He said that he did not love me anymore and was tired of pretending that this marriage was going to work.

I was currently renting a townhouse in a very nice section of a suburb of Washington, DC and was raising my three daughters and granddaughter alone. My oldest daughter got pregnant in 1992 when she was in her last year of high school. I chose to help her so that she could graduate and work to support her daughter, and contribute to our household financially. We were all adjusting well since the divorce and life seemed to be going quite well.

I was employed with the federal government and working in the Employee's Benefits Office. I assisted federal and military employees with retirement plans, thrift savings plans, health benefits, life insurances policies and compensations claims. I earned a fairly decent salary, but I was constantly looking for promotion opportunities to enhance our standard of living. I enjoyed working with the public. I was very personal and approachable with all recipients inquiring advice on such sensitive issues affecting their livelihood.

On Wednesday in October 1995 it was another ordinary day in the office. A male client (Clifford) came into my office around 10:30 am. He was about 5 feet, 9 inches tall, had a close fade hair cut, fresh shaven, and he wore fashionable eyeglasses. He wore a two-piece dark suit, with a white shirt and tie. He was dressed very professionally which meant he was a career man. What was most attractive about him was his smile which was soft and entreating.

Of course, I greeted him with a big smile and invited him to take a seat. He sort of joked about my last name and asked if I was related to the well-known singer Toni Braxton. I responded, "No, but my ex-husband is." Now that he knew my marital status, finding out his would be easy.

Clifford was approaching retirement status with the federal government in a couple of years and he needed to review his file to make sure everything was in order. While he sat in my office, I went to the file room to retrieve his employee record. I opened it and quickly scanned all the necessary information and on the surface everything looked okay. He was divorced, was currently working as a psychoanalyst and he earned a handsome salary. I also saw that we had something in common -- we shared the same birthday month, and his was the perfect age that I was looking for in a man.

Upon returning to my office, I gently handed him his file to review and told him to take his time. When he completed reviewing his file, he proceeded to ask me some questions about military benefits. He had served some years in the military before he entered the federal government. My knowledge was limited in this area, so I went to get my co-worker who could better advise him. They talked for a length of time while I listened and continued to check out this wonderful specimen that God created. I have to be honest – I had not seen anyone as handsome as Clifford in a long time.

Clifford seemed to be satisfied with all the information that he received, so my co-worker excused himself and went back to his office. It was past noon now and Clifford apologized for keeping me past my lunch hour; however, he did not leave immediately. We continued to enter into some casual dialogue. I mentioned that I noticed that his birthday month was the same as mine. We both exchanged the actual day we were born.

I liked him, and I liked the way I was feeling, yet I was afraid – afraid of being vulnerable again. I thought to myself, "I wonder where he is spiritually?" I wanted to know if he had a personal relationship with Jesus without boldly asking him. So I started to talk about my faith in Jesus. I knew for sure that this topic would either draw him in to a deeper conversation with me or quickly turn him off.

Clifford took an interest in my discourse and engaged me in a few questions about my faith. He said that he was saved but that he had never made a public confession. He admitted to me that he had a nervous breakdown in 1992 from the stress of his job and he was put in a mental institution. His thought pattern had become distorted and it was difficult for him to separate what belonged to him and what belonged to his patients. During his recovery, he invited Jesus into his life. I was touched by his testimony and we ended our visit.

He apologized again for keeping me past my lunch hour and gave me his business card before he departed. As he walked with slight pigeon-toes, each step he made was firm and full of life, and hints of the cologne he was wearing were left in the air.

When I scanned his business card, I did not think I would ever call him. A month went by and I remembered that Clifford's birthday, November 9, was approaching. I was contemplating if I should call. Well, I did and I left a birthday greeting on his answering machine. I purposely did not leave my number because this would cause him to come into my office again.

About a week later, Clifford walked into my office with that same soft entreating smile. This time he was dressed more causal in khaki pants, a striped shirt with an open collar and the cuffs rolled-up once, and shoes to match. Whatever he wore, you could tell it was good quality.

Of course, I acted as if I was totally surprised to see him. He thanked me for the call and apologized for not responding sooner. He said he was out of town on business and that he did not have my phone number to return my call. Therefore, he had to come to see me and get my number. We talked for a few minutes and he left with my number in his wallet.

Clifford and I did not talk again until New Year's Eve of 1995. I called him and invited him to go to church with me to bring in the New Year, but he said, he already had plans. We did however make a date to have dinner at my house and to meet my family the following week-end. My two youngest daughters did not warm up to Clifford initially because they were not ready to share me with anyone. My oldest daughter was happy for me because she had adjusted more quickly after the divorce.

Clifford started attending church with me. He was well received by everyone. He surprised me one Sunday when he went up during the altar call. Later, he told me his reason for going up was to publicly acknowledge his confession in Jesus Christ.

Our relationship seemed to be perfect. We were spending a lot of time together – planning fun and adventurous activities. Soon, Clifford began to talk about marriage. I was a little apprehensive, even though on one hand it was my heart's desire; on the other hand it was a big step! It seemed too good to be true and moving a little too fast.

My pastor and his wife counseled with us concerning the possibility of us getting married. They held mixed opinions. The pastor did not think that Clifford and I were spiritually compatible because of his relatively new walk in Christ. On the other hand, the pastor's wife saw the same thing, but she believed that God could do great things in and through Clifford as long he stayed yielded to the Holy Spirit.

I continued to walk by faith and kept every step before the Lord very prayerfully. I was happy but something in me was troubling.

One Sunday after church in January of 1996, Clifford said that he had something to share with me. I could tell it was difficult for him because he was quite nervous yet serious. As he was driving us back to my house, he confessed that he had filed for bankruptcy in 1993, and gave me all the details that led to his financial failure.

I exclaimed, "Is that all? I thought you were going to tell me that you were gay." He was relieved that I did not kick him to the curb, and I was relieved I did not have to kick him to the curb. We both had a good laugh. We talked about how I was good at managing finances and he agreed to let me manage the money.

As a matter of fact he said, "I don't mind if you are in the driver's seat. I interpreted this to mean that he did not mind me being in charge. This bothered me somewhat because I thought, "Why get married, if I had to remain in charge?"

Clifford said he wanted to propose to me in church before the congregation. He planned on doing this in April when we would have an engagement dinner. How romantic I thought! He seemed to be perfect. I thought he was the man I had been searching for. We would have stimulating dialogue which had a lot to do with the field of his employment. He was as supportive of my ministry, a teacher of Christian art to the Body of Christ, as I was of his work.

When people saw us together, they said we looked as if we were made for each other because he was so attentive to me. Clifford was also creative. He designed a discipleship program to implement in the church which would mend and restore family relationships. The pastor and his wife were very excited about what God was doing. Clifford and I decided that August was a good month to get married. We had six months to arrange all the plans. He started having money put into my bank account. Together we went and purchased a home to be built. The loan was in his name only because the requirement to be named on a government loan was that first I had to be married to him.

During one of our evenings together, Clifford was quite nervous again and said, "I have something to tell you."

I responded, "Okay" with a smile.

He exclaimed, "I am manic-depressive/bipolar."

"What is that?" I asked since I really did not know what this meant. He took a lengthy time to share what it was and the characteristics of his up-and-down behavior. Clifford's manic-depressive disorder was due to a chemical imbalance in his brain and he was on prescription medicine to control his mood swings.

This was my first experience with someone with this disorder. I now know that this was "the piece" of him that disturbed me. "What would I do when he was extremely depressed?" I thought. "How would it affect our relationship?"

"How would it affect our sex life, especially since I had been celibate for 6 years already?" Clifford also shared with me that impotency was a symptom of bipolar. I did not want to get married and continue to live celibate. The apprehension concerning his condition overwhelmed me.

Later, I realized that while Clifford and I were dating he was in the manic phase. These phases can last for several months or even years in some cases. He enjoyed showering me with gifts and I liked receiving them. He had gone shopping for himself one day at a local mall. On his shopping spree he discovered a lady's boutique that sold purses. When the sales lady showed him what she had in stock, he could not decide on which one he thought I would like, so he purchased five beautiful leather handbags. When Clifford presented them to me, I did not know how to respond.

As soon as I got through the initial shock, I exclaimed, "Oh, Clifford, what a nice surprise – five handbags! They are beautiful, but do you think I need five of them?" He replied, "It was difficult for me to choose when the sales lady showed them to me, so I told her I would take all of them."

I could tell by the look on Clifford's face that he was very proud of his act of kindness towards me. He stated that I could change purses any time that I got ready to go to an event. His expression was like a little boy. If I had rejected his gift, it would have crushed him.

Even though Clifford counseled people who had no order in their life, he too was chemically out of balance. He conveyed this story to me about his breakdown. He said, "I would see patients every day and help them with their problems. Many of my patients I had to admit to a mental institution for psychiatric care. I had internalized so much of their problems that I would take them home with me. Eventually, it was difficult for me to distinguish between theirs and my own. Then I ended up in the same mental institution with them." He also added with his soft smile, "I could see some of them asking themselves and others, while scratching their heads – isn't he the same man who counseled us and put us in here?" We had another good laugh.

Shortly after Clifford revealed his bipolar condition, I began to notice some slight changes in his behavior. He was not as talkative. He would stare at me and then bashfully look away when I talked to him. The vibrant life that I saw in Clifford the first day I met him was being slowly sucked out of him. He was not the same man as before.

Five months before our planned wedding date (March), I received my last phone call from Clifford. On the other end of the phone was the sound of a scared little boy, depressed and lifeless. He said he could not marry me or see me again because he was sick. This was incredibly devastating for me. It was as if I was having a nightmare and I wished that someone would awaken me. I cried for days until I was numb.

I hoped for a long time that Clifford would get better and come back into my life even just as a friend, because during our courtship we had become good friends. But he never did. Of course, I sent him a check to cover the money that he had given me; I could not take advantage of him. Looking back on all this now, I don't know how I recovered but only by the grace of God.

As I have described this courtship in its briefest details, all the signs pointed to this being God. I have often pondered! What I encountered seemed good to me from a natural standpoint but it was not God's best for me. God was perfecting all the details I did not see, to keep me from being trapped in a marriage that would have caused me excruciating pain – without a doubt – *Father knows best!*

There is a song that comes to my mind when I think about how God took care of me in this situation.

"Your Grace and Mercy"
Your grace and mercy has bought me through
I'm living this moment because of You
I want to praise You and please you too
Your grace and mercy has brought me through

The Fear Factor

It was January 2004. I and two other adults arrived a little early for our Faith Based Initiative class. This was our habit. Each of us enjoyed sharing with each other what had happened in our lives during the week. Soon the professor arrived and greeted everyone. She led us in prayer and class began.

The thought provoking question for the class period was "What will steal from the vision?" The look of eyes turning towards the ceiling in search of the answer to this intriguing question gave me a sense that everyone was asking what I was asking. I narrowed down the question as to how does this relate to Faith Based Initiative, which is the Church partnering with the community and the government to meet the needs of the community-especially the poor. As some of the students began to give intellectual answers (that I thought were good), I sensed that the atmosphere became charged with the presence of God.

Immediately my mind flashed back to when I was in junior high school, to when I got teased a lot during these early years of my life. These where formative years when the devil took unfair advantage of me and misrepresented me to my peers. The summer had ended and school was now in session. Students were piling in and finding seats; however, no one was rushing to sit next to me. At the age of thirteen I was obese and tilted the scales at 206, at only five feet, five inches.

I was told that I had a pretty face but was fat. I can laugh about it now, "I was pretty fat." At the time, it was no laughing matter. The devil had used my temporary obesity to his advantage and caused me to be timid and withdrawn. I knew I was fat and I did not need other people to remind me of it.

I was in an accelerated program with very smart students, but I did not feel smart at all. As a result, the struggle with insecurities hindered me from doing my best. I believe that a lot of my abilities were limited in junior high school because of the bill of goods (lies) I bought into from the enemy, saying that "no one likes fat people."

Before I entered into high school I had successfully lost all the excess weight and dropped down to 150 pounds. The progress of my weight lost even attracted looks from a very special boy who liked me. It felt good to be attractive to the opposite sex, in a good way.

Hence, intimidation shaped and ruled my entire life even after my weight loss. Oftentimes I wished someone would reach out to me and be my friend but being fat was not popular.

I remember stealing money from my mother to buy gifts for some of my classmates so they would like me. This was only a temporary fix. So I soon formed attitudes about my classmates and my race.

Through the years I became more withdrawn and internalized all of the hurt, pain and mockery my peers dealt to me. Consequently, I became a victim of my own abuse. I often isolated myself from other women, even those who did not judge me and wanted to embrace me.

The classroom became silent that day and I realized that everyone was waiting for <u>me</u> to respond to the question. Tears started to roll down my face and I could not prevent them from coming. God was up to something! The mind of God began to override my thoughts and I heard an inner voice speak to my spirit, "I am doing a redemptive work in you."

When I was able to voice my thoughts through all the tears and embarrassment, I said, "Intimidation will steal from the vision." Little did I know that this day was a day of new beginnings for me; I took all the limits off of God. I could have very well taken the path of least resistance. The pain and embarrassment of that season in my life was horrific. However, I allowed God to take me back and heal those inner hurts and close the door on that demonic plot forever.

That day in class the Lord revealed to me that I was living in the past. The lie that the enemy told me when I was in junior high school was keeping me attached to that horrific experience.

Unfortunately, I could not enjoy the present moment or go forth into the future, because I was stuck to the memories of my childhood and the devil used intimidation to keep me there.

Intimidation is a form of fear. Intimidate means to make timid, frighten, to discourage, to restrain or hold back or inhibit by threats. As I got older into my teens and up into my 40's, the devil used other women to intimidate me. Maybe, a particular woman was prettier than me, more outgoing, more intellectual or liked more by others. This would cause me to draw back and not embrace her. Then I would form an opinion about her and convince myself that she did not like me; therefore, I did not like her.

How can you not like someone that you do not know? **1 John 4:20** declares, **"If a man say, I love God, and hateth his brother, he is a liar: for he that loveth not his brother whom he hath seen, how can he love God whom he hath not seen?"** When you get the answer, let me know. I believe that this was a sophisticated scheme of the devil to keep me from giving and receiving support, encouragement, friendship, etc. from other women. Many negative things that control our lives can take on the form of fear. Its goal is to take power from us and prevent us from moving into our destiny.

I want to inform all women of one thing: You do not have to fear because God is with you! I have been delivered from fear and the spirit of intimidation and so can you! **"For God has not given us the spirit of fear but of power, love and a sound mind." (2 Timothy 1:7)**

Furthermore, the devil does not want us women to assemble together because when we come together on one accord (especially for the purpose of prayer) we are powerful.

Numbers 21:16 is very insightful to me, **"And from there they continued to Beer, that is the well where the Lord said to Moses, 'Assemble the people, that I may give them water.' "** I do not want to take this scripture out of context but I want to use it to illustrate a principle. Beer was a place or pit in the desert and at the time the Israelites had been traveling for a long time and needed water. Therefore, God instructed Moses to call the people together because He knew they needed water to help sustain them for their journey.

Many times I have seen another hurting sister in the Lord and neglected to reach out to her because of some negative opinion I had formed about her, or I wanted to remain self-absorbed in my own little world, and wanted to remain there rather than risk vulnerability.

Yet I said I wanted God to use me mightily! Our world gets bigger when we invite other people in. We must start out giving a cup to others, and then God will increase it to a gallon and a bucket. If we're faithful in a little, we'll be faithful in much.

Matthew 25:21: "His lord said unto him, well done, thou good and faithful servant: thou hast been faithful over a few things, I will make thee ruler over many things: enter thou into the joy of thy lord."

Ladies, we need to water each other! To water is a form of nurturing. We were created to nurture much more than men. Nurture means to give sustenance, to train, rear, educate, foster and cultivate. That is why God made women so important to men. Our sons need nurturing. We provide something that is necessary to their growth. Nurturing is an innate ability that women receive at birth. That is why we grew up playing with dolls and houses and not cowboys and Indians. We have the desire to provide care, and even need it at times. We need to be concerned about one another. We have the ability to give fresh perspective and encouragement to those who are feeling hopeless. The more we care about and serve others, the more the negative things in our own lives grow very dim.

Ladies, God's Word encourages us to embrace one another. Let's be approachable, and strive to be purifiers and not polluters. Master whatever insecurities you have because they are just **F**alse **E**vidence **A**ppearing **R**eal. Do not let them steal from the vision God has given you! Moreover, **1 Corinthians 10:13** declares, **"No temptation has overtaken you but such as is common to man; and God is faithful, who will not allow you to be tempted beyond what you are able, but with the temptation will provide the way of escape also, that you may be able to endure it."**

Something to remember: God can and will use our weaknesses for two reasons. First, He uses handicaps, hindrances and blunders to encourage the self-sufficient to rely on Him more. Second, He keeps us in touch with our limitations by empowering us in the midst of them so that we can do His will <u>in His way and in His strength</u>. This is just a nice way of saying, "Let go and let God!"

During my meditation time one morning, the Lord spoke these simple words to me: "The enemy has kept my women at bay too long; I am calling my women to come away from the bay into the deep waters to swim. When they come they will be able to take other women by the hand and keep them from drowning in their handicaps."

The Beginning of Birth Pangs

"For nation will rise against nation and kingdom against kingdom and in various places there will be famines and earthquakes. But all these things are merely the beginning of birth pangs." (Matthew 24:7-8) NASB

Have you ever been at odds with someone (whether a Christian or non-Christian)? On some occasions you have to discern who is sending or allowing the attack. Is it God or the devil? I just encountered a confrontation with a believer and my flesh wanted to let the person have their way, because I did not want to go through the battle. However, I had to get the mind of God and act accordingly. During the confrontation, God gave me the above scripture. I do not want to take it out of context, but the principle helped me understand why the conflict was so furious.

In February 2002, I had allowed this believer, who was a very close friend at the time, to use my credit card. I realized later that it was contrary to the will of God. This situation lasted for six years, because the other party was not fulfilling their end of the contract. It stole my joy and caused a root of bitterness to grow, which grieved the heart of God. Even though this contract was initiated by the other party, my willingness to enter into it hindered my spiritual growth significantly, and I could not go forth in ministry.

I had not realized the consequences of not thoroughly seeking the Lord before I allowed this believer to use my credit card. Because of the negative consequences that resulted from my ignorance in this situation, I became angry at this person.

It was of the utmost importance that I release my negative attitude and behavior towards this person. Yes, I had repented – and, yes, I confessed that "I forgive and release" this person every time negative thoughts came.

Of course, the devil did not want this to happen because he was happy that I was miserable. However, I was finally sick and tired of my current behavior and was praying for change. I had to accept the fact that no one is responsible for my happiness but me.

Now it was the beginning of birth pangs! The final payment was due in less than two weeks which would have been August 31, 2005. Paying this debt on the due day was always a challenge for this person. The greater challenge would be to get this person to honor the agreement and pay the full balance.

Like a pregnant mother in her final months, I was ready to get rid of the pain. Satan wanted me to stay in my present condition to birth an *Ishmael* (something that is not God's will), but I was determined that my *Isaac* (God's promise to me) would come forth. Even though the enemy became stubborn, God asked me, **"Will He bring me to the point of birth and not give me delivery?" (Isaiah 66:9)**

It seemed obscure as to how God was going to work out my situation, but I was only to believe that He was able and that He would release me. I was pregnant with the will of God and He was ready to bring it to fruition. This antagonistic element of resistance fought against me to cause me to abort the seed.

Well, the situation did not turn out the way the contract was written. As a matter of fact, the other person thought it was ridiculous for me to expect full payment when they did not have the money.

I don't think it is wrong to expect payment or full payment if the contract deems it so, especially if both parties agreed to the terms when the contract was initially written. **Psalm 15:4** states **"...He that sweareth to his own hurt, and changes not."** Somehow, we have interpreted this scripture to mean if it is not convenient to my present condition (regardless of the vow I wade to the other party) -change!

But God told me: **"If you just stand against the enemy of your soul, I will fight the battle and ensure you the victory."** Therefore, I stood firm during the entire confrontation. When the last attack came, I heard the Spirit of God say, "It is finished; I will take over now!"

When I heard this, I knew that something spiritual had taken place, because in the natural it was going to take another six months before this debt was completely paid. However, God's grace had abounded to me in such a way that I had a peace because He was in control.

Just like a pregnant mother who is in labor and exhausted from all of the contractions and physical pushing, and she eventually gives birth and finds out that there is something physically wrong with the child's lungs. The doctors inform her of the child's diagnosis. It is asthma! The problem is temporary though, because the child will eventually grow out of it.

The mother is sad but it is her child and she still loves the child. God gives her grace to walk through this disappointment. Her momentary affliction of pain and suffering, are working for her a far more exceeding and eternal weight of glory. **(2 Corinthians 4:17)**

Unfortunately, the outcome of my situation was difficult at the time. However, this was just another opportunity for me to trust God. During the next six to eight months, God worked total forgiveness in my heart towards this person and I am healed and free from all the pain surrounding this situation. I can truly confess that I am walking in wholeness. There is no amount of money in this world that can pay for a sense of well-being!

I have walked into my season! A season of increase and fruitfulness! Praise God! The seed that God has put in me has conceived and has now come forth. God desires the full weight of the seed (which is His glory) to appear. The seed will produce enough for me and for others. Now is the time for overflowing abundance.

God allowed the conflict to thrust me out of my comfort zone. Is He doing the same to you today, dear friend? I had become comfortable with being miserable. However, God wanted me to change. I was tired of my current situation and did not want to tolerate it any longer. God allowed insufferable pain in my life to arouse me to change. Is He doing the same thing in your life? If so, I encourage you to yield to the Holy Spirit and make the adjustments He is leading you to make.

No one desires to confront and battle the demons that need to be battled for change to occur in situations, and even those that lie deep within themselves – their own flesh. However, there are occasions we have to fight for change. Harriet Tubman, Rosa Parks, and Martin Luther King Jr., were all well known civil rights leaders who had to fight for a worthy cause that benefited many. I realized that my change was not just for me, but for all those who would eat of the fruit of my seed.

One of the reasons I believe that the Lord has led me to write about this situation is to encourage you to realize that your obedience to the Master's leading can be used to compel many others to change for the better to benefit not only themselves and their family, but the entire kingdom of God.

Control Freaks

"...Catch the foxes for us, the little foxes that are ruining the vineyards, while our vineyards are in blossom." (Song of Solomon 2:15) NASB

God has His way of getting at the root of our problems. As humans we only see in part, thus we usually deal with issues in a superficial manner. God's ultimate desire is that we be totally free of any hindrances and negative influences that will block Him from releasing His glory in our lives. It is often the small things in our lives which we don't see or which seem insignificant to us that will cause big problems if not handled correctly. As scripture illustrates above, it is the little foxes that spoil the vine.

At the time I was fifty, I had three daughters, one grand-daughter and a son-in-law, and we continued an old family tradition of getting together on holidays. Due to the modern day culture we live in today that tradition is loosing its grip on the family. Therefore, we make every effort to keep the family tides from becoming extinct.

New Years Day of 2006 was approaching and I was excited about going into another new year and expecting God to do extraordinary things through me. My family and I decided to celebrate and prepare a traditional New Year's dinner: fried chicken, collard greens and of course black-eyed peas. My middle daughter Lakisha, (enthusiastic and determined) would cook the black-eyed peas. This would be her first time making this dish. I pretty much approved of her being responsible for this task, but I was also anxious about it.

We were having several family members over for this particular holiday dinner and I wondered: Would she have them ready when everyone arrived and would they be cooked to perfection?

Therefore, I made some suggestions to assist in her cooking process. I did not convince her and eventually, she said, "Mom, I got this," in a sweet loving tone.

As she continued working in the kitchen, focusing on the step-by-step directions to the recipe, I was in turmoil over the preparation of the black-eyed peas. This was supposed to be a joyous occasion but I was unhappy. I asked the Lord, "Why am I struggling with this situation?"

I heard the Holy Spirit respond to me, "It's because you want to be in control." This was actually an eye-opener to me. Who, me…control?! The entire situation is funny now when I think about it; however, at the time I was ashamed of what I had heard because it was the truth. All I could do was agree, confess and repent to the Lord…and my daughter. As we engaged in discourse as she was cooking, she stated she was aware that I wanted control, but she held her position. Notwithstanding, my daughter did an excellent job, and the black-eyed peas were delectable!

This revelation from the Holy Spirit helped me to examine areas of my life where I was struggling in my relationships where there was interaction with God and people. I began to see more and more that I wanted to control them and different situations by insisting that things be done <u>my way</u>. I also began to see that this small insidious behavior, which was not so easily seen by my natural eye, but put under the microscopic eye of the Holy Spirit, can cause me grief and others pain.

It hinders me from having quality relationships in my life and those that are glorifying to God. We are to set an example for unbelievers and to exhibit behavior that makes them jealous. We should have such great relationships with our family members that they want to imitate. Doesn't scripture say that they will know us by our love for one another?

Also walking in love is a commandment, not a suggestion. When we attempt to control others, we are walking in the flesh, not in the Spirit and we need to recognize it as sin as God exposes it. When many of us come to the Lord, there are so many areas to be worked on, that He may not reveal it to us right away.

If the truth be told and you are honest with yourself, you, also have struggled with being in control. That is the quest of the human race. How can we control our environment, society, circumstances, etc.? We have a world full of "control freaks." Look at how many situations we have messed up because we did it our way. It's time to get out of the driver's seat and leave the driving to God! If we want God to use us in extraordinary ways in, we have to release the control and allow Him to be God in our affairs.

I am reminded of the hit song in 2005, Jesus Take the Wheel by Carrie Underwood, the winner of the American Idol contest that year. You are not alone in your struggle to let Jesus take over the wheel of your vehicle. Obviously many others are feeling this need also because it's evidenced by the hit success of the song. **Psalm 46:10** instructs us to **"Cease striving and know that I am God; I will be exalted among the nations, I will be exalted in the earth."**

Digging Broken Wells

"...Come. 'Let the thirsty ones come—anyone who wants to. Let them come and drink the water of life without charge.'" (Revelation 22:17)

I work as a DNA specialist at the Child Support Enforcement Office to administer genetic testing. Every week, I listen to many stories, tales, and lies from clients coming to our office for help. There are two sides to every story and everyone has one. I encounter angry, happy and mixed emotions from alleged fathers and I encounter mothers that come in with numerous children who all have a different father.

Many of these mothers do not see anything wrong with the way they are doing things. After months and sometimes years have lapsed, they come into the office to file a claim against the alleged fathers for child support. The reason I write about this is not to judge these mothers (because I also have three daughters who have different biological fathers) but to point out how an unsatisfied thirst can lead you to dig broken (anything that gives temporary comfort) wells. The wells can be wealth, social position, intellectual status, drugs or pornography or unhealthy relationships. The lack of my unsatisfied thirst being filled led me on a road to hell.

I was never one given to drugs or alcohol but I went from relationship to relationship to find comfort. The majority of the time, I was not looking for a sexual encounter, but just for some man to love and accept me and talk to me. On the other hand, they were expecting more than I wanted to give, so I submitted to having sexual relationship with them because I felt obligated to and felt it would keep them in my life. It is only the grace of God that protected me from getting AIDS.

The relationship I had with my father growing up was emotionally dysfunctional. For the most part he was physically present. My mother was the disciplinarian and my father was like a boy in a man's body. If I wanted to get permission to do anything, my father would always respond, "Go ask, your Mom!" I never really got the chance to really know my father on any kind of level. I saw what he did and what he did not do, I could recognize his voice, but I did not know his heart.

I desperately wanted his love and approval. I wanted him to dialogue with me, to play with me, and to give me advice about boys and life. I always admired and loved my father because that was what I was taught to do. I do not blame him for his lack of parenting skills since he grew up without a father (he never even met him during his entire life). He could not talk or write about his father, as I am doing about him today.

I believe that the void in my life caused me to dig broken wells. The void was not having a relationship with God and, in part, it included no knowing my father emotionally. In other words, I was seeking love and approval through unhealthy sources.

Some of the wells I dug were old and had stale water. I remember one in particular. I was 18 years old and in my first year of college, and the man I was seeing was twice my age. That didn't last long and once that one ended; I was seeking another relationship hoping that this one would quench my thirst and end my search.

I was like the Samaritan woman at the well, who had five husbands. On one particular occasion when she was thirsty she went to draw water from the well. She met Jesus who asked her for a drink of water and in turn she asked Him for a drink of the Living Water. His purpose for their encounter was to expose the root of her thirst. Just as this woman, I wasted precious time trying to quench my thirst and allowed myself to be a tool for another man's pleasure.

John 4:7-10: "There cometh a woman of Samaria to draw water: Jesus said unto her, 'Give me to drink.' (For his disciples were gone away unto the city to buy meat.) Then said the woman of Samaria unto him, how is it that thou, being a Jew, ask drink of me, I am a woman of Samaria? For the Jews have no dealings with the Samaritans. Jesus answered and said unto her, 'If thou knew the gift of God, and who it is that said to thee, Give me to drink; thou would have asked of him, and he would have given thee living water.'"

John 4:15-18: "The woman said unto him, Sir, give me this water, that I thirst not, neither come hither to draw. Jesus said unto her, 'Go, call thy husband, and come hither.' The woman answered and said, 'I have no husband.' Jesus said unto her, Thou hast well said, I have no husband: 'For thou hast had five husbands; and he whom thou now hast is not thy husband: in that said thou truly.' "

It would have been wonderful if I had realized how negative the consequences of my traveling on this path would be. Having sex outside of marriage was advised against by my mother and other Christians, but this course of action seemed to at least, in part, temporarily satisfy the deep longings of my soul.

However, it took many years before I recognized I was really searching, in part, for a spiritual father who could protect, care and mentor me. Another reason I believe it took so long is because I did not think the way I was going was really that wrong – regardless of how many times the path I chose ended in a disaster.

I know better now, because wisdom comes with age and as Ray Charles used to say in the Pepsi commercial, "You got the Real One now baby!" The Real One I have is Jesus, the same One whom the Samaritan woman met. As she was thirsty due to another broken relationship, I was thirsty again for true inner peace, love and approval.

I wish I could say that once Jesus saved me when I was just a little girl, my search ended. However, I remained thirsty and had a certain amount of unrest in my soul for many years after I rededicated my life to Christ at the age of 26. I was now married, provided for, working in a good job, had well-behaved children and was attending a good church. There was still no one to help me get to the core of my problem, and as a result my marriage soon began to break down.

My husband was just as thirsty. We were not able to meet each other's deep needs due to our emotional dysfunctions and insecurities.

I came to truly understand my thirst in 2005. I was set up by God. A seminar was being hosted by a church I used to attend. Those that had attended this seminar before me were returning with testimonies of how this three-day seminar had changed their lives. I was happy for them but I was still not convinced to attend.

One day I was approached by one of the attendees who inquired why I had not registered for the seminar. I told her and God used her as the catalyst to get me to the seminar.

The facilitator was extraordinary in his teaching style. He was not a psychoanalyst, but he could have stood toe-to-toe with one any day. He was a Christian, businessman, and minister and his training was founded on Christian principles. I was captivated by his knowledge of the human psyche.

After three days of boot-camp training, I left knowing who I was, I understood my thirst and I was determined to press on towards the high call of God for my life.

My academic study since then, in clinical counseling, has helped crystallize what God started in that seminar. I know it is okay to be thirsty because that thirst was put in me by the Lord. I do not have to dig broken wells anymore because I drink from the well of Living Water. Jesus was always there for me, but I did not think He could satisfy my thirst. How silly! If Jesus is author of my thirst, He is the only One who can satisfy it. Today, my heart is burdened for the mothers and alleged fathers who come into my office. The majority of them are young, and they do not have anyone to explain to them the deep longing of their souls. I do not know how their lives will end. Prayerfully, some will find their way and change their course of direction. However, some may continue going in the wrong direction. But, to those who are tired of digging broken wells and ready to drink from the Living Water, I leave the words of this song of God's redemptive grace.

"Come just as you are
Don't you hear the Spirit call?
Come just as you are
Come and see, come receive
Come and live forever
Life everlasting
Strength for today
Taste the Living Water
And never thirst again.

Issues of the Heart

"The heart is deceitful above all things, and desperately wicked: who can know it?"(Jeremiah 17:9)

We had a problem with moths in our kitchen pantry in the home I had resided in for the past eight years. We were constantly killing them, thinking each time the problem was solved. Soon, we begin to see some larvae and we became alarmed. We called in an exterminator to examine the areas. It was bad news! The inspector could not just spray the pantry with some insecticide to destroy them. We had to throw away all boxed food and wipe clean every can and the entire pantry with bleach and water.

The inspector also informed us that what we were visibly seeing was a result of microscopic moth eggs that would hatch into larvae and then into moths. Not until the inspector examined the pantry did we know what to look for or how to treat the problem. We could have reached for a temporary solution, such as bug spray and thought we were resolving the problem, but because we weren't really getting to the root of the problem, our efforts were in vain.

This situation is similar to how a root problem in me caused me to exhibit negative behavior throughout most of my life. My outward behavior and attitude did not line up with the Word of God, because of what was going on in my heart. If your physical body is wounded, it is not going to function properly. No matter how hard a person tries to do things with a broken arm, they're going to have several limitations. Similarly, if a person has a broken spirit (heart) it dries up the whole body. **"A sound heart is the life of the flesh: but envy the rottenness of the bones." (Proverbs 14:30)**

As a child, the issues of my heart did not seem to matter as much because my parents disciplined me according to my behavior and attitude, and that was the end of it. For years, the issues of my heart were overlooked and dismissed. Yet, I was disciplined for the same disobedience over and again. The issues of my heart became a nuisance when I was forced to take responsibility for my bad behavior and attitude towards people. Therefore, how did all this come about? Here's my theory or what I believe the Lord showed me.

From the time I was in junior high school until I moved out of my parent's house on my own, I saw my mother strike out at my father, once or twice a month. It was usually during my father's pay period. My father worked at the post office as a security guard, and he made very good money. The problem arose when he would go out with his friends and spend his entire paycheck drinking and partying with his girlfriend. Unfortunately, my father often made bad choices and the entire family suffered as a result.

Of course this would infuriate my mother and she would attack him physically, which was her way of releasing her anger and demanding that he not repeat this ridiculous behavior. I believe the pain and disappointment of my father's recurring irresponsible behavior caused my mother to develop a demanding spirit. My mother was a good and loving woman, but she believed she did not have to tolerate this ill-treatment. My father would never strike back at my mother because he was afraid, so he would respond by leaving the scene.

As a matter of fact, my mother was like the disciplinarian and my father was like the child in their relationship. I did not have bad parents. They raised me and my other siblings in the best way that they knew how. They fed, clothed and provided shelter for us. They did not physically abuse or mistreat us.

However, they had wounds from their childhood. They were weak in relationship skills as they never saw proper ones modeled. They never got healed from the wounds and hurts of their heart and that caused them heartaches in their marriage.

This childhood memory had a huge impact in the way I dealt with people. My mistakes were based on the choices I made. I believe I made choices based on the information that was registered in my subconscious mind, which included pictures of my childhood incidents without discretion. Therefore, I operated a lot out of my subconscious mind which had an archive of past files even though I did not realize it at the time.

For example, if I was struggling in a relationship, the file that best suited the struggle was retrieved and applied. Most of these files could not be trusted, because they were damaged with pain and disappointment. My struggles had a lot to do with the inner hurts and wounds of my heart, and other people were never the real source of my problems. I *wanted* them to be, because this would take the attention off of me and place the blame on them.

When I started working on my doctoral degree, I was assigned to read books by Dr. Larry Crabb. He is a Christian psychologist, who wrote books about human relationships. This was the avenue that the Holy Spirit used to reveal the origin of my relational problems. I had held onto anger towards my father for how his behavior affected our family, especially my mother. She was very hurt by his behavior, so I shared her pain as a child and into adulthood.

I believe this offended spirit caused me to be impatient and critical with people. I wanted things done a certain way and I expected it, as my mother did in her relationship with my father. If it did not go according to my plan, then I had something to complain about. Usually what I had to say was on the borderline of corrupt communication – murmuring, grumbling and complaining!

Unfortunately, I followed my mother's footsteps, and developed a demanding spirit, and operated in the sin of self-protection. The sin of self-protection is all about protecting yourself from getting hurt again, which is impossible. We build up a defense and isolate ourselves from people. This goes against the will of God. Jesus was hurt more than anyone in this world and He never isolated Himself from humanity. He was always open to minister to the vilest person, if the Spirit was directing Him.

As a child, this sinful pattern of behavior was inbred in my subconscious mind. I did not strike out physically to others as did my mother, but I would withdraw and not speak, hoping that my attitude would make the other party feel guilty - manipulating them into doing what I wanted them to do. This was my way of getting what I wanted.

I was definitely operating in the sins of my mother. Unfortunately, whether conscious of it or not, I modeled the type of behavior I saw my mother operate. It clearly became my pattern of behavior exhibited for most of my life as I interacted with people.

If I was fulfilling my end of the agreement, then the other party should equally fulfill their end. Legally and biblically, this is correct. However, everyone does not live according to the same standards, and I have learned that I cannot force anyone to do what is right.

At the age of fifty, the light was turned on in the dark places of my heart. It was so horrifying that I cried every day for two weeks. The thought of hurting the Lord was painful. Jesus was the standard by which I was judged, and I did not meet it. Jesus never used manipulative behavior to get what He wanted. He allowed people to choose.

Jesus was aware that Judas was stealing money from the money bag that was entrusted to him. Jesus was never offended or tried to protect Himself from

Judas. Jesus also knew that Judas was going to betray Him. Jesus never stopped loving, giving or sharing fellowship with him. He never demanded an answer from Judas, saying, "Why did you do this to me?" In the end, Judas was sorry unto tears, but he did not know that he could be forgiven. Well, I can replace Judas' name with my name.

Over and again, I have violated the law of love when I operate in the sin of self- protection. God never meant for me to be an island to myself. He created me to be part of a body, working together. Occasionally, another member of the body may hurt and disappoint me; however, my duty is to forgive and love him or her unconditionally. I have also violated the law of love through the sin of demanding, which caused me to manipulate via tears, seducing words or actions. First Corinthians chapter thirteen is the love chapter and if you study it you will discover that you also have violated the law of love.

I am a person of influence which means to impact, but when influence turns into control, I have lost the power to impact effectively. God created all men with a free will. I was not created to try or attempt to control another person's will or vice versa. I must accept him or her for whom they are in the spirit of love. If what they do or say offends me, then I must first look within my heart and ask myself, "Why did I get offended or why am I so touchy?"

When someone gets easily offended or over reacts to a situation, it's been said they're usually not reacting to today's offense, but to yesterday's offense. Majority of the time it is a build up that occurred even 20-30 years ago. It's like the analogy of the straw that's breaking the camel's back. **"Great peace have they which love thy law: and nothing shall offend them." (Psalm 119:165)**

The Bible declares that the heart is deceitfully wicked and God is the only One who knows the evil that we are capable of committing. Our daily prayer should be, **"Create in me a clean heart, O God; and renew a right spirit within me." (Psalm 51:10)** and **"Search me, O God, and know my heart: try me, and know my thoughts: And see if there is any wicked way in me, and lead me in the way everlasting." (Psalm 139:23-24)**

Conclusion

I have experienced the good, the bad and the ugly; however, there was always sufficient grace available to me. I have been up and I have been down; by all means, up is better. The beauty of it all is to learn to draw on the grace of God in the midst of the fiery furnace, to realize that God is actually not only for me at the time, but Jesus is also with me and actually in me and that because of that power with me I can endure the heat of the oven and walk out unharmed.

One of the major ways I have come to learn to draw on the grace of God in the midst of trials is to first of all change my perspective or way of looking at any particular situation, refuse to allow any thoughts contrary to God's Word to dwell in my mind.

It is not enough to disciple my mind not to think negatively. I have to put positive thoughts in my mind instead. Therefore, the next step is constant meditation on God's Word.

To behold my trials and tests with a new outlook was enlightening and gratifying to my spiritual growth. Life may not have been fair, but God was always just in His dealings with me. I leave you with these powerful words of the Apostle Paul: **"No temptation has overtaken you but such as is common to man; and God is faithful, who will not allow you to be tempted beyond what you are able, but with the temptation will provide the way of escape also, that you may be able to endure it. (1 Corinthians 10:13)**

Bibliography

[1] The Complete Word Study Dictionary: New Testament, Chattanooga, TN, AMG Publishers, 1993.

[2] Andrew Murray Daily Reader, Minneapolis, MN, Bethany House, 2005.

[3] Matthew Henry's Commentary, Grand Rapids, Zondervan Publishing House, 1960.

[4] Bible Discovery Library Program, Translations, KJV, NASB, iExalt Electronic Publishing, Austin, TX, 2005.

About the Author

Coraleen is a licensed evangelist of the gospel of Jesus Christ and has spiritual covering under Pastor Decker Tapscott, of Faith Christian Church, International Outreach Center in Warrenton, VA.

Coraleen has a prophetic anointing and has been called as a teacher for these end-times. She teaches Sunday school and discipleship class. She is known for her ability to instruct in a practical way.

Coraleen holds a Masters of Art in Christian Education where she was recognized as Valedictorian. She also holds a Doctorate of Ministry from Faith Christian University and Schools and Seminary.

Coraleen has three daughters--Carmelita, Lakisha, Nichelle; a granddaughter, Racquel; and son-in-law, Malcolm.

Mailing address:
10723 Norman Ave.
Fairfax, Virginia 22030
703-934-4755
Email: Coraleen111@aol.com

Printed in the United States
99235LV00002B/1-15/A

9 780979 808418